Bobcat

by Robert Bridges
illustrated by Meryl Henderson

Core Decodable 24

I0806528

McGraw Hill Education

Bothell, WA • Chicago, IL • Columbus, OH • New York, NY

MHEonline.com

Send all inquiries to:
McGraw-Hill Education
8787 Orion Place
Columbus, OH 43240

ISBN: 978-0-02-135337-8
MHID: 0-02-135337-9

Printed in China

6 7 8 9 10 DSS 27 26 25 24 23

Look! A bobcat is on a cliff.

It sits on a flat rock.

Can it look at the fat rabbit?

A bobcat sniffs a rabbit.

A bobcat can look fast.

Look! A bobcat can stand stiff.

A bobcat sprints fast!